THE WORLD'S BEST

BEACH
HOUSES

THE WORLD'S BEST
BEACH
HOUSES

edited by Mandy Herbet

images
Publishing

Published in Australia in 2012 by
The Images Publishing Group Pty Ltd
ABN 89 059 734 431
6 Bastow Place, Mulgrave, Victoria 3170, Australia
Tel: +61 3 9561 5544 Fax: +61 3 9561 4860
books@imagespublishing.com
www.imagespublishing.com

Copyright © The Images Publishing Group Pty Ltd 2012
The Images Publishing Group Reference Number: 1046

National Library of Australia Cataloguing-in-Publication entry:

Title:	The world's best beach houses / edited by Mandy Herbet.
ISBN:	9781864705003 (hbk.)
Subjects:	Vacation homes.
	Seaside architecture.
Other Authors/Contributors:	Herbet, Mandy.
Dewey Number:	728.72

Edited by Mandy Herbet

Designed by The Graphic Image Studio Pty Ltd, Mulgrave, Australia
www.tgis.com.au

Pre-publishing services by Everbest Printing Co. Ltd., in Hong Kong/China

Printed on 140 gsm GoldEast paper by Everbest Printing Co. Ltd., in Hong Kong/China

IMAGES has included on its website a page for special notices in relation to this and our
other publications. Please visit www.imagespublishing.com.

Contents

Introduction

Mandy Herbet // Editor

There's nothing quite as relaxing as being by the water. To me, the beach evokes memories of long, lazy summer days spent on the hot sand, waiting for the next ice cream or a chance to run into the waves and cool down. A time when rest and relaxation ruled the roost and everyday stresses had no place. As the projects in this book reveal, this evocative memory is not restricted to any one country and we're proud to be able to feature superb beach houses from around the world.

These projects all embody the lazy days of summer in their own way. They face different oceans and different horizons but they all share a link to their surroundings. Some of the houses have been purpose-built and others have been renovated to fulfill their new owners' needs, but all are connected to the landscape. With views of the ocean from almost every corner, these houses reflect their environment and our love of the beach.

Many of the architects faced huge challenges in designing these houses – difficult sites, local government restrictions or existing structures. Building on small plots without access or under conservation protection tests design in many ways but you'll be amazed at how the architects featured overcame these elements to design beautiful spaces that embrace the environment.

The beach is often a place where nature meets man-made and these houses reflect that relationship. Using a combination of man-made and natural materials, some of these houses are designed to blend into the landscape entirely – clad in local timber designed to grey and match the natural environment, or built entirely into the landscape itself – while others are intended to stand out as a testament to modern design, with steel and glass framing magnificent ocean views.

Designed to celebrate their position, these houses allow the owners to be at one with the landscape – infinity pools are cantilevered over cliff-faces and all-encompassing views celebrate their enviable beachfront positions. While many of us only associate the beach with summer, these houses are designed for year-round enjoyment. During the summer, the open-plan living and expansive decks embrace the natural breezes and long days and during winter, the indoor and outdoor fireplaces create a warm and inviting space, combating bleak winter days. These are truly enticing spaces.

I hope you enjoy paging through this compilation of the world's best beach houses and that they evoke the same memories of lazy days filled with sun and surf as they did for me.

A Classic Backdrop

USA // Estes/Twombly Architects

The surrounding countryside of this waterfront location is classic New England, typified by bucolic open fields bordered by stone walls. The programme for this project included an open floor plan, private master and guest bedrooms, and space for a significant collection of paintings and ceramics.

The outbuildings comprise a two-car garage, a barn for the owner's skiff, wood shop, and storage areas. Only a small portion of this 2.8-hectare (7-acre) site was suitable for building – a gentle knoll that constituted approximately six percent of the total area. However, this section of land also afforded panoramic views of the ocean and nearby protected wetlands. The architect used the knoll as a plinth for a cluster of small buildings – a living area, bedroom, garage and barn. These buildings were pushed to the edge of the plinth and linked with a wall of local granite to help distinguish man-made and natural forms as well as manicured and un-manicured yards.

Durable metal roofing and deep overhangs protect the traditional cedar siding and painted trim. Large expanses of glass enclose the entry hall and wrap corners to capture sunlight and views. On the interior, detailing was kept simple and straightforward, with the palette of materials and subdued colours intended to serve as a backdrop for the owners' furniture and art.

Photography by Warren Jagger Photography Inc.

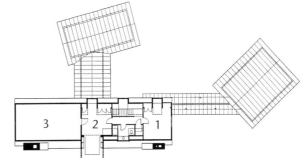

1 Bedroom
2 Bedroom/study
3 Attic storage
4 Wood shop

First floor

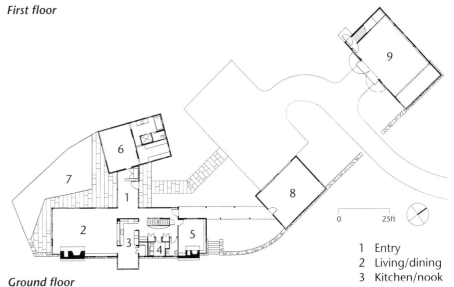

Ground floor

0   25ft

1 Entry
2 Living/dining
3 Kitchen/nook
4 Laundry
5 Study
6 Master bedroom
7 Deck/terrace
8 Garage
9 Barn

11

A Flawless Transition

Brazil // Bernardes Jacobsen Arquitetura

Built among sand dunes on a beachfront site, this 185-square-metre (2000-square-foot) house was positioned to take advantage of natural ventilation and the spectacular sea views. The structure incorporates a variety of indoor and outdoor spaces that allow for a seamless transition to the beach and sufficient room for an extended family to relax in a casual atmosphere.

The main building is connected to the sandy site by a concrete base and the rest of the structure is built from timber. The main area comprises a large living room that has unrestricted views to the beach and garden and has been positioned to ensure that natural sea breezes flow through the space. All other rooms of the house flow from this main living space.

In response to the tropical surroundings, a palette of materials was selected to help the house blend harmoniously with its environment. Locally sourced materials include eucalyptus used for the trellis detailing and beige Bahia marble for the floor coverings. This marble, which is a similar shade to the surrounding sand, is also used for the solarium and beachfront swimming pool.

Photography by Leonardo Finotti

First floor

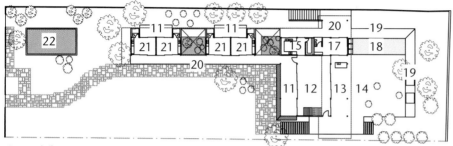

Ground floor

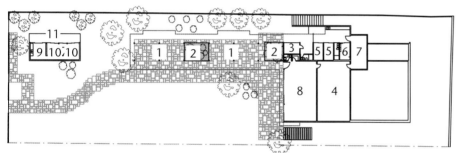

Lower ground floor

1	Garage	14	Sunroom
2	Garden	15	Kitchen
3	Sauna	16	Pantry
4	Storage	17	Living
5	Staff bedroom	18	Pool
6	Laundry	19	Deck
7	Services	20	Circulation
8	Children's room	21	Ensuite bedroom
9	Kitchen/living	22	Rooftop garden
10	Bedroom	23	Study
11	Verandah		
12	Living/dining		
13	Covered verandah		

A Modernist Icon

USA // Studio 9one2

Sometimes, good things come in small packages. This house started out as a small package. The lot, 9 x 18 metres (30 feet x 60 feet), was the product of some odd property subdivision early in the last century. Bordering on a 'walk-street' and surrounded by other houses, this lot had no vehicle access and, consequently, no garage. It was only buildable because of a grandfathered zoning rule that permitted it. Facing a walk-street on one side and The Strand on the other in Manhattan Beach, this lot was one of the most precious un-built pieces of real estate in Southern California. The client was a bachelor who wanted a showcase home in a high-profile beach town location. He selected Studio 9one2 for their innovative designs and experience working on beachfront homes on difficult sites.

Studio 9one2's design approach was to create a space that incorporated ocean and beach views, as part of the living space. With a house of just under 100 square metres (1000 square feet), the design parti was driven by the need to create the illusion of more space than there really was. Architect Patrick Killen placed all the public living spaces at the front of the house to capture the panoramic views and placed the private spaces within a series of concrete walls toward the back, thus establishing a strong connection to the beach and the ocean, just steps away. Two-storey walls of glass stared brazenly at the beach and ocean while simple bush-hammered concrete walls modulated the more private parts of the house and provided both structural support and separation from adjacent houses. Killen separated the house from The Strand and walk-street by placing it on a tapered dais and created a miniature front patio defined by a 1-metre-high (3-feet) semi-circular fence. He designed an oversized roof cap with a weatherproof Zincalume fascia to give both a visual definition of the house's footprint and modest sun control.

Incorporating the two themes of sea and sand, Killen used the building's colours and textures to remind us of the surroundings. The sand colour and texture was repeated in the bush-hammered concrete. The deep blue tint on all the glazing controls the intense sun and gives the ocean a refreshing colour, even on grey days.

Studio 9one2 considers this one of their finest works and numerous design awards have confirmed this. Being in Los Angeles, the house is often the venue for fashion photo shoots and charity galas. On one of Manhattan Beach's most prominent corners, Studio 9one2 has created a 'Modernist icon' that will stand the test of time.

Photography by Dean Pappas

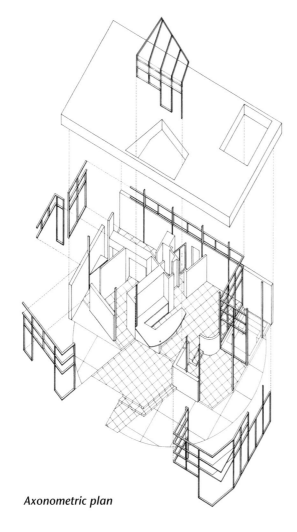

Axonometric plan

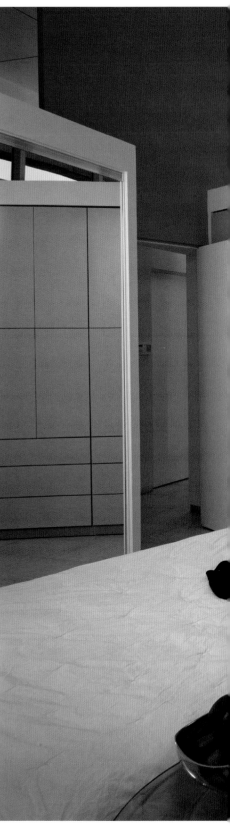

A New Form

Australia // Paul Uhlmann Architects

Surrounded by palatial homes, many of which are three and four storeys, this beach house is relatively modest by comparison. 'In an area of brand new homes, the original 1980s home was probably one of the oldest,' says architect Paul Uhlmann, who recently redesigned this house with a more contemporary edge.

Originally designed to accommodate two families who could live independently from each other, the brief was to create one home. The original houses were completely detached, with a central courtyard connecting them. A number of walls were demolished and the courtyard was completely transformed. A plunge pool (complete with a square porthole window) was designed for the courtyard, framed by a river-stone wall. A significant part of the courtyard was also enclosed with full-length opaque glass doors. Now used as a secondary living area for the family, it's difficult to imagine the home's original structure. 'We wanted to retain part of the courtyard. The southeasterly trade winds can make the conditions on the beachside quite blustery. It's important to have an alternative outdoor area for four to five months of the year,' says Uhlmann.

The 1980s home had a low ceiling. Currently, in part of the informal living area, which faces the beach, the ceiling height is only 2.7 metres (9 feet). 'I like this scale. It creates a sheltered feeling from within. There's a sense of intimacy,' says Uhlmann. However, to make the most of its idyllic position, Paul Uhlmann Architects installed large timber and glass sliding doors that can be completely pulled back. The side glass-louvred windows can manipulate the prevailing winds. To compensate for the low roof and to give the home a new focal point, the architects included four recycled-timber beams on the beach façade, which also provide structural support.

While the house is often occupied by more than one family, the spaces can now be shared by everyone.

Photography by David Sandison

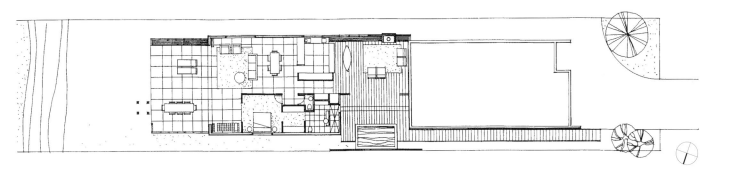

A Panoramic View

Australia // SJB Architects and SJB Interiors

Few beach houses enjoy such a privileged position. A mere 25 metres (80 feet) from the water, this house overlooks grassy sand dunes. Designed by SJB Architects and SJB Interiors, the new house is one of a handful along the water's edge. Replacing an old beach shack with a new house gave the architects an opportunity to match the design with the location. The focus is on the beach, the bay and the sand dunes.

The owners, who have grown-up children, not only wanted a design commensurate with the view, but also a house that could be used when the children weren't there. In response, the architects created two living zones that could be occupied independently of each other.

On the top floor are the main bedroom, ensuite, kitchen and living area. On the ground floor are three bedrooms, main kitchen and living area. Both levels have generous access to the outdoor areas. On the ground level, the walls of the house are extended to frame the outdoor areas, creating privacy and protection from the wind. On the second level, there is a continuous outdoor deck that wraps around the entire space. While the outdoor space, framed with glass balconies, appears exposed to the elements, a retractable awning on the roof can be used for protection.

The façade is clad in western red cedar. Crisp and contemporary, it presents a modest face to the street. However, once through the front door, full-length glass windows face the view. As architect Alfred de Bruyne says, 'the design celebrates the position. It's a regular-sized block, but you don't feel as if you are hemmed in. The neighbour's front gardens are part of the larger picture. You could be simply anywhere.'

Photography by Tony Miller

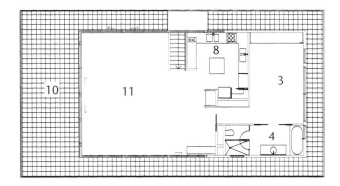

First floor

1   Verandah
2   Entry
3   Bedroom
4   Ensuite
5   Bathroom
6   Laundry
7   Store
8   Kitchen
9   Recreation room
10 Terrace
11 Living/dining

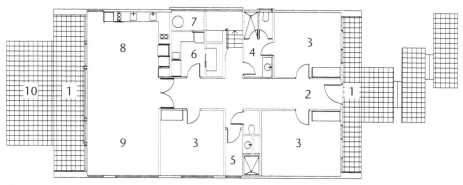

Ground floor

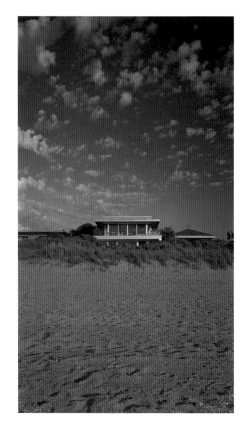

A Rural Location
Scotland // studioKAP

The site of this single-family dwelling, a rural location on the west coast of Scotland, commands a wonderful aspect southwest across Loch Melfort to the Isle of Shuna, Croabh Haven and beyond. Seen from the water, the site is contained to the left by a small, tree-lined burn and to the right by the dirt road leading down to a massed concrete pier. Curving around the back of the site is the embanked coastal road.

As the location is highly exposed to the open sea-loch, the architect's primary considerations involved developing a strong link between building and landscape. With this in mind, a dialogue was established between house and pier in terms of opposition, orientation and materials. The beach is a place where the natural and man-made meet – driftwood lodged among rock, pier cast over a rocky skerry – and the design of the house overtly recognises this. Materials are self-finished and durable, responsive to changing light and landscape but also acknowledging local traditions from a non-traditional position, down on the shoreline.

In the internal composition, the overriding theme was the resolution of exposure and shelter, namely how to provide the latter without diminishing the former. Both excitement and refuge are provided for and massively thick, creamy walls are played against cool grey windows. Through the plan and sectional composition – conceived as a held bunch of flowers – an inevitable journey towards the sea continues, passing by shady caves and through sunny volumes.

Photography by Keith Hunter

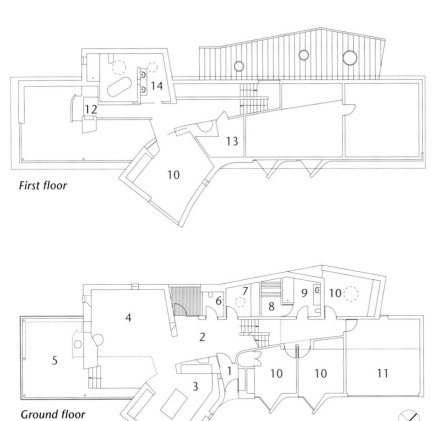

First floor

Ground floor

1 Entrance
2 Reception hall
3 Kitchen
4 Main living area
5 Sea room
6 WC
7 Utility
8 Sauna
9 Shower room
10 Bedroom
11 Garage
12 Study
13 Store
14 Bathroom

A Seamless Living Experience

Turks and Caicos Islands // RAD Architecture, Inc.

Located on the east coast of Providenciales, this 697-square-metre (7500 square feet) Barbadian-style beachfront vacation villa sits on a beachfront lot of just less than a hectare (2.5 acres). Interior and exterior spaces flow seamlessly into one another to create a magical indoor outdoor beach living experience.

The architect's aim was to create a home where a couple, family or group could be equally comfortable. The design includes large, open spaces for large groups to congregate, but equal attention was also given to smaller, more private areas for individuals or couples to enjoy solitude throughout the day. This was achieved by creating four separate pods of living areas, securely linked through open-air travertine galleries. These elegant covered halls feature traditional floor-to-ceiling aqua-coloured wrought-iron gates and Tuscan columns entwined with night-blooming jasmine and stephanotis from the bordering gardens.

Three of the four pods contain four bedrooms and the other central pod houses the kitchen, great room and library on the upper level and an additional bedroom, games room, laundry and cistern on the lower level. The main master bedroom pod sits atop the two-car garage and pool pump room. Each of the upper bedrooms overlooks the infinity-edge pool to the crystal clear azure waters of the Caicos Bank.

Photography by www.provopictures.com

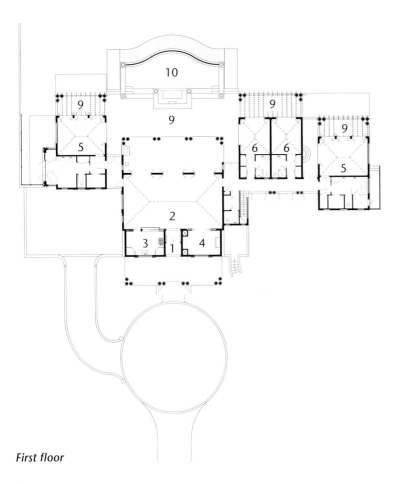

First floor

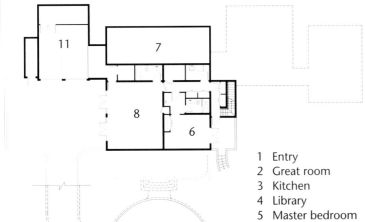

1 Entry
2 Great room
3 Kitchen
4 Library
5 Master bedroom
6 Bedroom
7 Cistern
8 Games room
9 Porch
10 Pool
11 Garage

0   10ft

Ground floor

A Sense of Permanency

Australia // Robert Andary Architecture

In contrast to many lightweight fibro beach shacks, this house offers a sense of permanency. Constructed of concrete and glass, the two-storey rectangular design hovers above the dunes and gnarled coastal scrub. The client wanted a showpiece that embraced the site as well as the ocean views.

The house has two sides and frames two different views. One façade features concrete and rectangular glass windows, in firecrest-orange and clear glass. The alternate façade, facing the sea, has floor-to-ceiling windows and doors leading on to an expansive deck. 'The house doesn't really have a back or a front. There is a road on both sides that leads to the front door,' says architect Robert Andary, who embraced the site with extruded forms (the upper-level extends 30 metres — 100 feet).

The ground level, which acts as a plinth for the upper level, includes a garage, two bedrooms, a games room and a bathroom. There is also a covered courtyard, with an elliptical glass roof. On the upper level are the kitchen, dining and living areas. At either end of this space are two bedrooms, both with their own bathrooms. For privacy, the two bedrooms can be completely screened by large sliding doors. Alternatively, these bedrooms can be opened up to the main living areas, becoming an extension of the open-plan space.

While Andary describes his work as the interaction of two simple rectangular forms, it is, in fact, a highly considered and masterful design. The swimming pool, for example, cantilevers over the dunes, appearing as a black box on a façade. The design included a glass wall in the concrete façade and aligned the pool to embrace the ocean beyond the living room. 'When you're in the pool, you feel as though you are swimming out to sea,' says Andary, who also integrated an elliptical glass skylight in the courtyard into the living room floor. A timber walkway slices through the house to meet the deck on the other side of the house.

Photography by Tony Miller

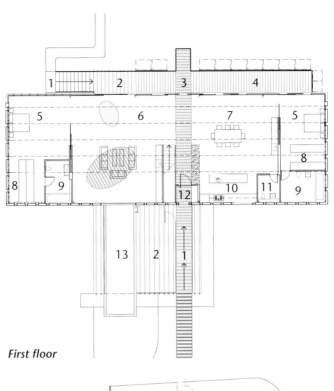

First floor

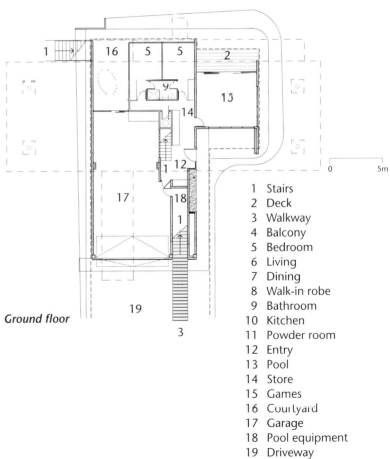

Ground floor

1   Stairs
2   Deck
3   Walkway
4   Balcony
5   Bedroom
6   Living
7   Dining
8   Walk-in robe
9   Bathroom
10 Kitchen
11 Powder room
12 Entry
13 Pool
14 Store
15 Games
16 Courtyard
17 Garage
18 Pool equipment
19 Driveway

A Union with Nature

Australia // Artichoke Design Studios

The owners of this beach house, on the central coast of New South Wales, explored the coastline from Victoria to Queensland. 'They were looking for a site with superb ocean views, with access to a beach. They were keen to avoid suburbia at all costs,' says architect Robert Pullar, director of Artichoke Design Studios.

While Pullar's clients found their ideal site, they were faced with numerous constraints, including a 30-degree slope. 'It's quite a difficult site. There were also additional restrictions imposed as it bordered a national park,' says Pullar. A large sandstone boulder in the centre of the triangular shaped block compounded constraints on the eventual design.

The house was constructed of reinforced concrete slabs, steel poles and glass and is clad with compressed fibre cement sheeting. 'The choice of materials was largely guided by the proximity to the national park. The materials had to be fire-resistant. There also had to be provision for water tanks and an elaborate sprinkler system,' says Pullar.

The house was designed for a city couple wanting a weekend retreat for themselves as well as a place to entertain friends and family. 'In order to determine the best possible orientation and floor levels to maximise the views, I set up a 4-metre (13-foot) trestle ladder at various positions on site,' Pullar says.

As a result, views can be enjoyed from every level of the multi-level home, whether at garage level, or from the main bedroom and study located on the highest level. There are even spectacular views of the ocean from a fully glazed staircase that leads to an open-plan kitchen, living and dining area on the second level. However, one of the best aspects in the house is from the ensuite through to the main bedroom, which offers ocean views, as well as views of the coastal gums.

Outdoor decks also play a major role in the design of this house, due to the incline of the site. As Pullar says, 'You can go down to the beach. But you can more than enjoy it all from up here.'

Photography by Alan Chawner

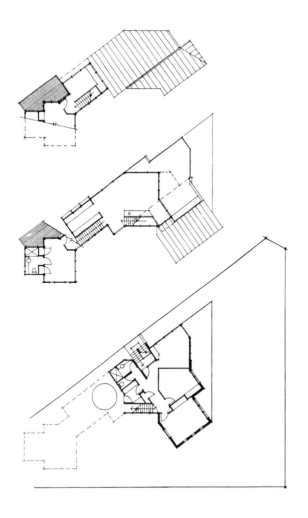

Ablaze with Colour

USA // Alexander Gorlin Architects

This striking, 1115-square-metre (12,000-square-foot) modern summerhouse is set on a narrow spit of land between the ocean and the bay. While simple in form, the house is rich in texture, colour and detail, with African teak offsetting pale limestone. Created for a family of four, the house comprises three master bedrooms, three guest suites, staff quarters and 557 square metres (6000 square feet) of living and entertaining areas.

At the entrance, the second floor cantilevers outward from the principal mass of the building in a bold formal gesture, creating a sheltered patio adjacent to the main entry. From here, an open staircase rises through a double-height glass atrium to the main level. Inside, the house is organised around a large, open living area. A central fireplace subtly partitions the space, creating an informal dining room to one side and a sitting area to the other. A light monitor in the ceiling above adds volume to the space and washes the room in a diffuse light.

The living room opens onto a terraced patio and pool beyond. Above, a great wing-like canopy extends from the building, shading the house. In marked contrast to the substantial mass of the limestone building, this finely tapered form floats above the patio. Clad in a soft grey metal, it seems almost to disappear against a pale sky. The pool looks out toward the ocean while a wooden boardwalk traces the gentle rise of the sand dunes, leading to a private beach below. A rooftop terrace offers spectacular views of the ocean and the sound. Bold sculptural elements clad in a pale metal punctuate the expanse. Their surfaces – grey and flat in the morning light – take on a warmer hue as the sun rises in the sky and at sunset they are set ablaze with colour.

Photography by Michael Moran, Esto

First floor

1 Gallery
2 Bedroom
3 Bar
4 Cabana
5 Living
6 Dining
7 Kitchen
8 Master bedroom suite

9 East terrace
10 Office
11 Sunroom
12 Upper terrace
13 Pool terrace
14 Spa
15 Pool

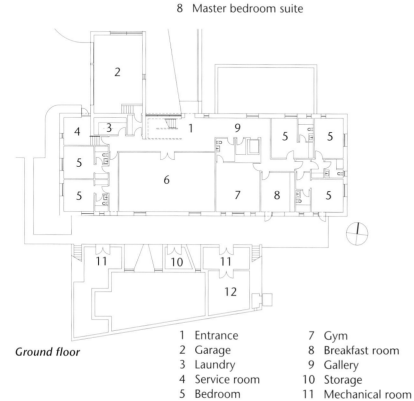

Ground floor

1 Entrance
2 Garage
3 Laundry
4 Service room
5 Bedroom
6 Media room

7 Gym
8 Breakfast room
9 Gallery
10 Storage
11 Mechanical room
12 Pool equipment

An Homage to Simplicity

Malta // Architecture Project

The challenge presented by this project was to convert two original apartments – characterised by labyrinthine differences in levels, curved steps, colonnade partitions and a compartmentalised plan – into one new open-plan living space.

The typical apartment layout consisting of a corridor with rooms leading off it was discarded and, instead, different spaces were linked together simply by exploiting the flow of natural light. The main living spaces all connect to the central core of the apartment, which houses the kitchen and dining area. This area anchors all of the other main zones: the living quarters, the master bedroom, the second and third bedrooms, and the guest bedroom and utility area.

Continuity was established throughout by creating broad sightlines and expanding openings, allowing the optimum amount of light and ventilation to filter through. Materials and textures play a significant role in the apartment, allowing the positive aspects of the space to be thoroughly optimised. Features such as semi-opaque glass, reflective surfaces and light colours allow light to penetrate every corner of the apartment, while sliding doors and ceiling-high units ensure abundant storage space throughout. The units also act as dividers for the rooms, articulating the space accordingly.

The primary aim of this design was to create a home specific to the clients' needs and tastes and this meant completely rethinking the original space. The new apartment needed to be light, clean and, most of all, an homage to simplicity. The result is a living space in which a dead end will never be encountered. Instead, there is an element of hiding and revealing, a focus on the combination of utility and luxury as well as extreme complexity in the achievement of simplicity.

Photography by David Pisani, METROPOLIS

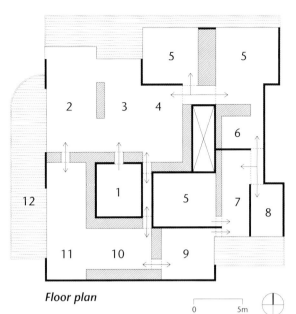

Floor plan

0   5m

1 Entrance
2 Living
3 Dining
4 Kitchen
5 Bedroom
6 Bathroom
7 Gym/spa
8 Laundry
9 Master bathroom
10 Walk-in robe
11 Master bedroom
12 Terrace

An Unforgettable Landscape

Mexico // Girvin Associates and Manolo Mestre

Located just north of Puerto Vallarta, Mexico, Palmasola was built as a private residence on just under 1 hectare (2.25 acres) within the Punta Mita Resort. Comprising 11 separate structures in a tropical, village-like setting, the residence offers 2322 square metres (25,000 square feet) of spacious living on a pristine beach.

Flanked by a Jack Nicklaus Signature golf course and a Four Seasons Hotel, Palmasola's authentic Mexican architecture and classic tropical landscape provide an unforgettable setting. A 61-metre-long (200 feet) undulating infinity-edge pool provides security and visually connects outdoor spaces to the Pacific Ocean. Stepping-stones float across the pool surface and provide access to the beach and a romantic dining palapa.

Lush, tropical landscaping offers privacy and shade from the hot Mexican sun while creating and separating outdoor spaces. Meandering walkways, stands of mature planting, and stone walls direct views and provide intimacy throughout the site, taking advantage of the 'borrowed' landscape to give the compound scale and context. Service paths are strategically located to provide separation from primary circulation corridors.

Photography by Michael Calderwood and Mark Callanan

At One with the Sea

Indonesia // Graham Jones Design/Manguning Architects

A 3-metre-high (10-foot) stone wall is all that separates the stunning Villa Surgawi from the ocean on Bali's central east coast. Located at the end of a beach shared by local fishermen and holidaymakers, this minimalist contemporary villa is a structure at one with the sea. The magnificent coastal scenery of islands, palm trees and beaches seems almost to envelop the home. This connection is particularly evident in the large timber deck straddling the swimming pool that cantilevers out over the sea wall beyond the boundary of the property.

This private residence comprises two separate pavilions, staff quarters and a guest cottage. A master suite and home office are positioned in a gabled roof pavilion on a flat section of the site, excavated for the pool and outdoor entertaining area. An internal stair provides access up into the main pavilion, which houses the kitchen, dining and living areas. On the upper floor the pavilion opens out to a balcony overlooking the ocean to the west, and timber decks at ground level open to the south. The building protects these decks from the occasionally harsh coastal climate, yet the transparent design ensures the views are uncompromised. A tropical garden at the front of the villa leads via white palimanan stone steps to a solid timber gate at the street-level entry.

Photography by Gali Gali

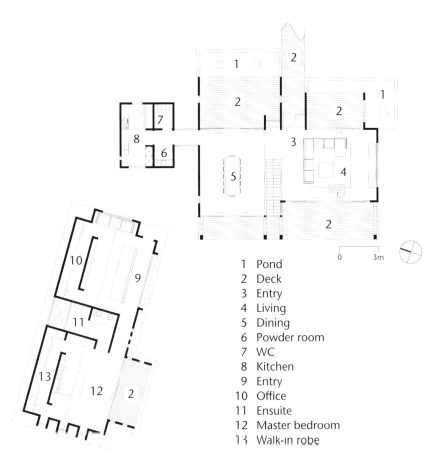

1 Pond
2 Deck
3 Entry
4 Living
5 Dining
6 Powder room
7 WC
8 Kitchen
9 Entry
10 Office
11 Ensuite
12 Master bedroom
13 Walk-in robe

At the Water's Edge

New Zealand // Craig Craig Moller Architects

This weekender is located at Paihia, Bay of Islands, in New Zealand. The house sits on the edge of a secluded bay, a short walk from the local shops. 'The owners have teenage children. They liked the secluded position, but they didn't want to have to be constantly driving their children places,' says architect Gordon Moller of Craig Craig Moller Architects.

Originally natural bushland, the local area was subdivided into 15 allotments. While this site is closest to the water's edge, it is also one of the steepest sites, with a gradient of approximately 15 metres (50 feet). This slope, along with the local weather conditions, informed the design, a three-level timber home. 'Our clients wanted something that could also accommodate guests, with their children regularly having friends to stay,' says Moller.

The entrance and garage to the beach house is on the top level. This level also includes three bedrooms and a shared bathroom. A staircase leads to the middle level, the most impressive of the three. This area features a winter garden that is flanked by the kitchen, dining and living areas on one side, together with an expansive timber deck. On the other side of the winter garden or atrium are two bedrooms, one being the main, and the other for guests. And on the lowest level is a second living area that doubles as a bunkroom, should additional friends stay over. The lower level is linked to the main living areas via a small set of stairs, similar to a ship's ladder.

The arrangement of the timber decks was important in the design. 'When it's calm down here, the doors can be pulled back and the breeze gently comes through the house. But it can become quite bleak, particularly during the winter months,' says Moller, who designed an outdoor fireplace on one deck for the colder days.

Clad in cedar board and batten, the house is understated. Some floors feature polished concrete, while others have polished timber. The interior wall finishes are also modest, many of which feature whitewashed plywood. As Moller says, 'It's about the surrounds and the pleasure of interacting with them.'

Photography by Simon Devitt

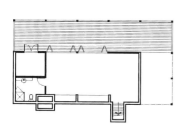

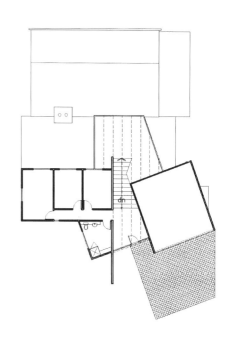

Balanced between Forest and Sea

Canada // Helliwell + Smith: Blue Sky Architecture

Planned as a grand, sweeping crescent-shaped structure opening to spectacular vistas north over a pebble beach, this house and studio was built as a gathering place for an extended family living in England and Canada. While the convex side flows along the shoreline, the opposite, concave side of the plan creates a courtyard that embraces the southern sun.

The sculptural timber roofs float above the walls of glass and cedar. Exposed glulam beams curve through the space, supporting a series of undulating rafters that define and form the roof and highlight the circulation gallery. The curved beams tie into vertical concrete fins, which are exposed on the interior and clad in large bluestone slabs on the exterior. The interior is sparsely detailed and constructed with materials including hardwood floors, architectural concrete and bluestone.

A transparent link of folding glass walls forms a hallway across the outdoor room and creates an illusion of two homes: one for the parents and one for the children. A series of 1.5-by-3-metre (5-by-10-foot) pivot doors open onto the seaside of the main social spaces. The plan arcs continue outside as unifying landscape elements, tying together the buildings, gardens, forest and sea. Great attention has been paid to details and craftsmanship resulting in a beautiful home balanced sensitively between the forest and the sea.

Photography by Gillian Proctor and Peter Powles

Blue Sky and Ocean
Australia // Odden Rodrigues Architects

The house is only an hour's drive south of Perth's CBD, part of an emerging outer suburb. Overlooking Avalon Point and with views to the Indian Ocean, the house is slightly oriented to the northwest with unimpeded views.

While the house is on the fringe of town, it still enjoys unspoilt coastal heath and dune vegetation. The brief to the architects was for a simple and sturdy house for a couple with three young children. According to architect Simon Rodrigues, 'they wanted something quite robust, like many of the homes built in the 1960s and 70s. They didn't want a townhouse on the coast.'

While it isn't made of fibro cement and perched on stilts like homes of that period, the house is relatively simple, both in form and materials used. Made from concrete tilt panels, galvanised steel beams, concrete floors and a steel roof, the house extends over three levels. Part of the ground floor is nestled into the sand dunes, with half this level almost submerged. This bunker-like area includes storage for rubber dinghies, fishing gear, a pool table and car parking. Craypots and an endless number of surfboards are also housed in this area.

The first level, oriented to the beach, contains five bedrooms, including the main bedroom that leads to a terrace. To maximise views, the living areas are on the top level. The open-plan kitchen, living and dining area includes dramatic picture windows. Divided by a viewing platform that's accessed by a ladder, the vista includes a rich palette of blues, from the ocean to the sky.

This beach house has a strong industrial aesthetic. Floors are concrete, as are many of the walls and some of the doors are made of steel. 'The owners found many of the fittings in second-hand yards,' says Rodrigues, pointing out the stainless steel basins in the bathrooms. Some of the artefacts, such as the art in the living area, once appeared behind a hotel bar in Perth. 'The house is really quite restrained. I didn't want the house to compete with this view. It's essentially the blue sky and the ocean,' says Rodrigues modestly.

Photography by Robert Frith

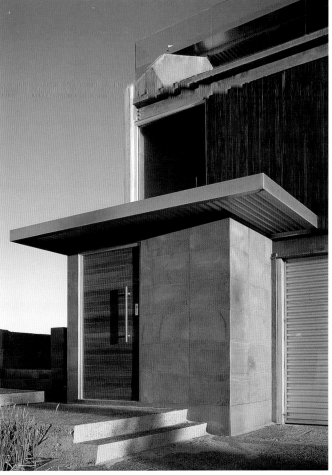

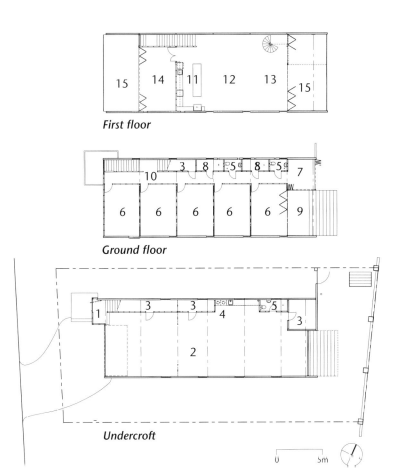

First floor

Ground floor

Undercroft

0   5m

1 Entry
2 Garage
3 Store
4 Laundry
5 WC
6 Bedroom
7 Sunroom
8 Shower
9 Deck
10 Hallway
11 Kitchen
12 Dining
13 Living
14 Rumpus
15 Balcony

Connected to the Landscape

Italy // Gabbiani & Associati

This holiday house is on Albarella Island, a small privately owned island south of the Venetian Lagoon, between Venice and Ravenna. The island, connected to the mainland by a private causeway, comprises hotels, private villas, a sports centre and beach and golf clubs.

Taking advantage of the double waterfront site, the house is split into three interconnected volumes. Seamless integration between indoors and outdoors is achieved through wide glass walls, and continuity of flooring and finishing materials. Each of the three volumes connects with its surrounds through a different approach, depending on its orientation, the type of landscape it overlooks, and its function.

The western volume, which connects with the nature reserve, houses the living quarters on a single floor composed almost entirely of glass walls. The double-height entrance volume acts as a type of hinge between the other two areas. The two-storey eastern volume, the furthest from the water, contains the sleeping quarters and bathrooms. The curved roof forms integrate gracefully into the landscape, recalling the shape of the sand dunes on the Adriatic coast.

Photography by Arnaldo Dal Bosco and Gabbiani & Associati

Connecting to the Sea

Australia // Wright Feldhusen Architects

This house appears to merge with the sea. 'Our client is a keen swimmer. He wanted to be connected to the water, whether he was doing laps or relaxing inside,' says architect Tim Wright.

While the house enjoys 180-degree views of the water, there are houses directly in front. But as the house is perched on a hill with a 6-metre (20-foot) fall of land from front to back, the vista isn't compromised by neighbouring homes. Relatively modest in size, the 500-square-metre (5400-square-foot) site was subdivided by the owners.

Designed for a couple with two young children, the house is spread across three levels. Car parking and servicing equipment for the pool are at basement level. The kitchen, living and dining areas, a children's rumpus room, plus a guest bedroom and ensuite are on the first floor. On the second and top level is the main bedroom, dressing area and ensuite, as well as the children's bedrooms and laundry. As the site slopes towards the street, the laundry is aligned to ground level. Whether you're in the main bedroom or in the living areas, water can be enjoyed from most vantage points. 'Our clients wanted the house to be as transparent as possible,' says Wright.

To achieve this transparency, the house features extensive use of glass. Zinc cladding and off-form concrete also make up the range of materials used. Zinc, being a non-ferrous material, resists rust – essential for being so close to the sea. 'The off-form concrete was poured to appear as though it had grown out of the site,' says Wright, pointing out the horizontal bands of concrete that form the base of the house, as well as in the walls of the double-height void enclosing the staircase. 'Our clients wanted a house that was low-maintenance. But the house is fairly exposed, so concrete anchors the house to the site,' says Wright.

One of the most pleasurable activities for the owners of the house is using the pool, either for laps, or just for splashing in. 'You feel as though you're swimming out to sea,' says Wright, who cantilevered the main bedroom approximately 2 metres (6.5 feet) to strengthen the connection between house and water. 'It's only a rocky outcrop below. So the pleasure of the beach comes from gazing out through these windows.'

Photography by Olivia Reeves

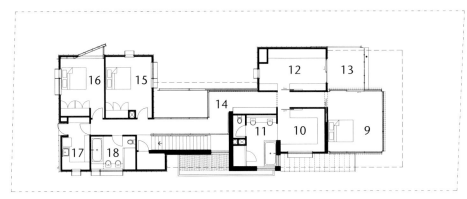

Upper floor

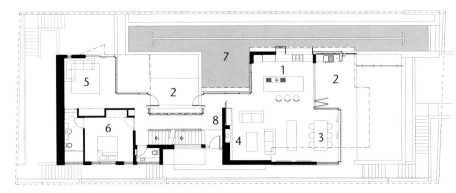

Ground floor

1 Kitchen
2 Terrace
3 Dining
4 Lounge
5 Play room
6 Guest
7 Pool
8 Entry
9 Master bedroom
10 Walk-in robe
11 Ensuite
12 Study
13 Balcony
14 Gallery
15 Bedroom 2
16 Bedroom 3
17 Laundry
18 Bathroom

0   5m

Contemporary Mediterranean Spirit

Italy // M. Campi, L. Giusti (gbc architetti)

'Pure and contemporary' was the brief provided by two young Neapolitan professionals who wanted to renovate their International style family villa, less than an hour's drive away from the city, and create a summer shelter and place for relaxing weekends.

The result constitutes a mix of contemporary design and Mediterranean spirit in keeping with the wonderful surrounding island landscape. Indeed, the panorama of Capri seems to enter the apartment and play a role in all of the important spaces.

The barycentre of the house is undoubtedly the great living room, which looks like a platform over the sea. A spectacular glass window frames the vista of the famous Faraglioni stacks and Marina Piccola bay in its entirety. This perspective of the sea constitutes an element of such beauty and fascination that it became the generating point of the entire spatial layout. All rooms participate with and enjoy the constant presence of the sky and the sea.

The metaphor of the sea can also be found in the furniture, much of which is architect-designed. Dynamic geometries – offering surfaces to support the television and other audiovisual equipment – symbolise the bridges of great ships, and combined with the large, panoramic windows create the feeling of being in a luxury cabin of a great cruise ship.

Photography by Mario Ferrara

0 2m

Cooled by Sea Breezes

USA // Hammer Architects

This five-bedroom home is located on a coastal dune overlooking Cape Cod Bay. The design consists of comprehensive renovations and additions to a single-storey 1960s modern house. The existing 2.8-square-meter (30-square-foot) footprint and foundation could only be altered on the non water-facing side, as the original structure was built within a 30-metre (100-foot) environmental conservation easement area.

The first floor was renovated to provide a living room, family room, dining room wing and screened porch. The lower level includes a suite of three children's bedrooms and a playroom. Additional space was accommodated in the new second storey, which comprises a master bedroom suite with its own private deck, guest bedroom and home office. The smaller square addition on the front side accommodates the new interior stair and entry. An outdoor stair from the bluff was constructed to access a private beach.

The sunscreen structure shades the double-height living space and reduces heat gain, thereby eliminating the need for air-conditioning and significantly reducing energy consumption. Operable windows, sliding doors, and skylights permit natural ventilation by prevailing sea breezes, cooling the house.

Photography by Bill Lyons

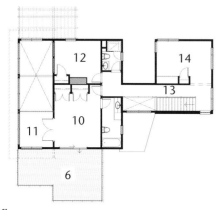

First floor

Ground floor

1	Living	8	Storage
2	Kitchen	9	Outdoor shower
3	Dining	10	Master bedroom
4	Breakfast	11	Balcony
5	Screened porch	12	Bedroom
6	Deck	13	Hall
7	Study	14	Office

Designed for the Weather

Brazil // Humberta Farias

Together with Olga Wanderley, architect Humberta Farias designed this house on 2000 square metres (21,528 square feet) of land, surrounded by an ecological reserve. On one side there is a coconut tree jungle and, on the other, a large native swamp.

Using her main style characteristics – regionalism mixed with modern – Humberta designed the house's structure in concrete and used local materials for the exterior and interior finishes. Thus, the wooden roof is covered with clay tile, rushes are found in many parts of the house and the bricks are largely from the local area.

Using the 'sea star' as inspiration, the house forms a clear geometric volume with defined lines, and this shows up in the surrounding context. The house is divided into two different blocks, with the main body featuring two floors and a leisure area surrounding the swimming pool.

The main access is on the swamp side together with the swimming pool area. A sauna, kitchen aid, a barbecue area, the service area and the shade for the swimming pool and the garages complete this area.

The main block is 450 square metres (4845 square feet) where the ground floor provides the social areas, which are distributed throughout a large and wide saloon. A common and informal meeting place, characterised by a brightly coloured Brazilian fabric motif, can be found on the middle floor. The bedrooms are on the upper floor. They share the mezzanine's large hall where there are stairs and a connection from the lower level to the upper level.

Everything was planned to lessen the impact of Alagoas' warm weather. Many rooms are designed in a way to receive the region's prevailing winds and to take advantage of the sunsets.

Humberta Farias shows particular flair for interior design and makes a special effort to include the region's crafts in her designs, involving the creative talents of the local people. One can see in this house the architect's principal characteristics: the concern for incorporating the landscape, and attention to the client's satisfaction.

Photography by Rogerio Maranhao

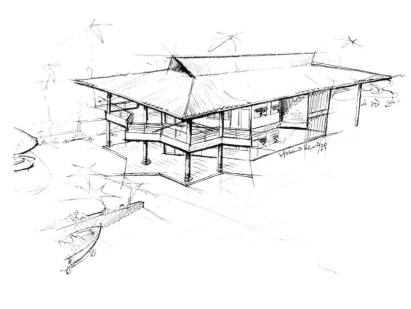

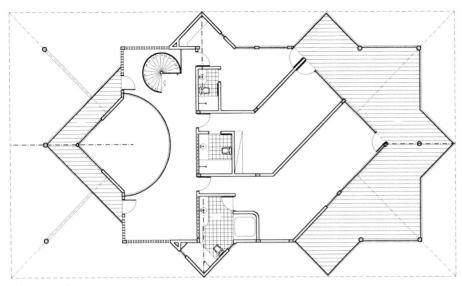

Upper level

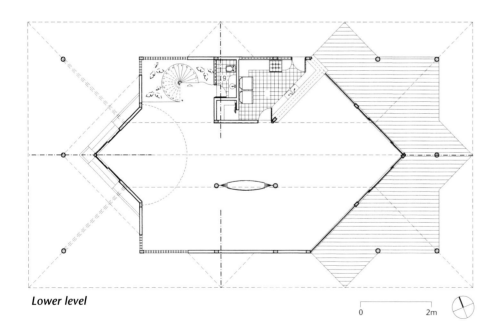

Lower level

0   2m

Designed for Two or Four
Australia // Centrum Architects

This beach house at Lorne, Victoria, was designed for a couple with adult children. 'Our brief was to design a house that would work for the whole family or just for two people,' says architect Ken Charles, who worked closely with fellow Centrum Architects directors Geoff Lavender and Alan Cubbon.

Overlooking Loutitt Bay, the site is as much about the shoreline as the hilly bush setting, dominated by established eucalypts. As the slope of the site is approximately 30 degrees, the materials used are fairly lightweight: timber and steel frames clad in Ecoply and solid timber straps. Painted a purple-red hue, the Ecoply evokes the colour of a sunset at Lorne.

Because of the steep slope, almost two-thirds of the land couldn't be built on. However, to maximise the building envelope, the house is spread over three levels. The top level, also the street level, includes a 'platform' for the parking of two cars, a study and entry vestibule. One of the most distinctive features upon arrival is the sculptural staircase made of timber, glass, painted board and steel rods. Like the angular posts at the top of the staircase, the timber feature wall is also angled. 'The angles were a response to the angled branches of the trees. They're quite dramatic,' says Charles, who placed a slot window at the top of the staircase and generous glazing below.

On the central level of the house, an open-plan kitchen, living and dining area all benefit from panoramic views of the trees and water. There's even an impressive view of the water from the ensuite to the main bedroom, fulfilling the brief for water views from every vantage point.

Timber features extensively in the interior of the home. Recycled timber was used for the flooring in the dining area, extending to the outdoor terrace. There is also extensive timber joinery, such as a credenza built into the living area.

On the lowest level, designed with separate access, are two additional bedrooms, a bathroom, a billiard room and gymnasium. There is also a second living area. 'The two floor plates are almost identical. The two areas can be used in their entirety or partially closed down if the owners come down on their own,' says Charles.

Photography by Axiom Photography + Design

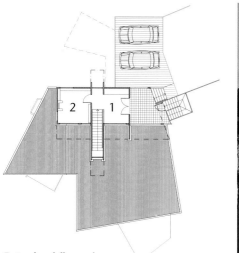

Entry level floor plan

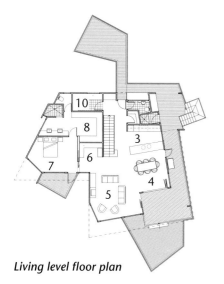

Living level floor plan

Lower level floor plan

1 Entry
2 Study
3 Kitchen
4 Dining
5 Living
6 Bar
7 Bedroom
8 Dressing-room
9 Games
10 Laundry
11 Gymnasium

Designed from Afar

New Zealand // Daniel Marshall Architect

The architect of this house in New Zealand didn't meet the owners until the house was being constructed. At the time, the owners were living in the United Kingdom, planning a return to New Zealand to live permanently. The design evolved by phone and the internet. The final stages relied on an animated film on DVD, together with a physical model of the house, shipped over to the UK.

The initial brief for the house at Omaha, an hour's drive north of Auckland, was Cape Cod style. 'It wasn't a style our office is known for. We prefer creating contemporary homes,' says architect Daniel Marshall. As a way of finding a compatible path, Marshall suggested the owners look at a book on the architecture of the Hamptons in Long Island, New York. 'Many of these homes are quite contemporary,' he adds.

The site, perched above the beach, was also influential in the design. Because it is relatively exposed to the southeast winds, the architects felt a protected courtyard space was required. As a result, the glass and cedar-clad house features a courtyard garden, protected from the wind by a single-storey living pavilion. 'We wanted the owners to be able to look though the living areas to the sea, rather than feeling closed off,' says Marshall.

On the ground floor are the kitchen, dining and living areas, together with a second raised sitting area. The two living areas are separated by American oak joinery, one side functioning as storage, while the sitting area on the other side includes an open fireplace. At the front of the house, facing the street, are three bedrooms and a bathroom. 'You can see the water from wherever you are in the house,' says Marshall, pointing out the vista from one of the bedrooms.

On the first floor are the main bedroom and ensuite, together with a dressing area. There is also a separate bunkroom. Marshall included a balcony, accessed via the main bedroom, to allow the sea views to be enjoyed at all times. 'It's a reasonably transparent house. The coastal dunes are integral to the design,' says Marshall, who included glass sliding doors in most rooms.

While the house isn't Cape Cod style, there are finely sculptured nooks in the essentially rectilinear form. The cedar plywood ceiling in the sitting area is faceted. And three smaller canopies protruding over the deck have a fine sense of craftsmanship. 'It is contemporary, but it's not just a minimal glass box,' says Marshall.

Photography by Daniel Marshall

Designed in Three Dimensions

USA // Studio 9one2

This avant-garde beach house is a seminal work for Studio 9one2. It marked a design breakthrough for architect Patrick Killen and put him on the map as the 'leading residential Modernist' on the west side of Los Angeles. Studio 9one2 was approached by a couple with children, who owned a beachfront property in Manhattan Beach, looking for a beach house that was 'avant-garde'. Killen's earlier work at the beach had given his client confidence that he could create the dramatic house they desired.

As with all beachfront lots, the size and setback requirements presented a constrained building envelope. Killen's solution was to use the lifeguard stands, just yards away, as a design inspiration.

He took the lifeguard stands' 78-degree windows and mimicked the shape by designing a canted fin wall that bifurcated the front elevation. Working from either side of this wall, Killen hung balconies and bays that projected rakishly toward the ocean. To add some visual excitement, Killen designed three large green glass sconces and placed them on the edge of the fin wall. Internally, the wall was repeated in art glass and stainless steel, separating the atrium from the dining room. This art glass and stainless wall is also a water feature.

Unlike many architects, Killen designs in three dimensions. Taking the 78-degree theme from the elevation to the plan level, Killen rotated the entire structure 12 degrees, offset from the property lines and placed third-storey balconies and bays at the same rotation. This subtle shift improved ocean views and separated the house from its close neighbours. On the main floor, Killen gave the house a grand curved staircase constructed of steel and glass. The steel frame was painted with an automotive finish giving it a durable and glowing look.

Using simple but durable materials, glass, stainless steel and stucco, Killen created an eye-popping, exuberant, Modernist building in a sea of sameness. With awards and press to follow, Studio 9one2's avant-garde beach house established Modernism as a viable architectural motif on the western edge of Los Angeles.

Photography by Dean Pappas and Holly Stickley

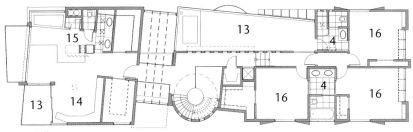

Second floor

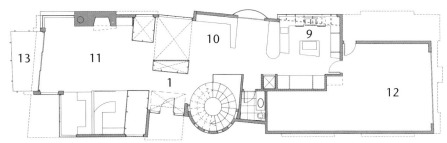

First floor

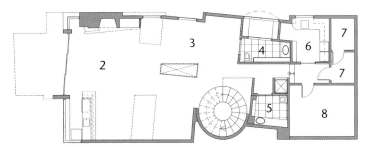

Basement

1 Entry	9 Kitchen
2 Family room	10 Dining
3 Exercise room	11 Living
4 Bathroom	12 Garage
5 Powder room	13 Deck
6 Laundry	14 Master bedroom
7 Utility	15 Master bathroom
8 Storage room	16 Bedroom

Designed on a Fault Line

USA // Studio 9one2

The client for this breathtaking Malibu house was an entrepreneur, real estate developer and triathlete. He purchased this 1 hectare (2.2-acre) site along the Malibu coastline with the desire to build a home with exceptional views, framed by exceptional architecture. The only drawback of the site was a major seismic fault line, which ran right through the property. Most coastal Californians live within striking distance of major fault lines, but few actually live right on top of them. Not to be deterred, architect Patrick Killen set out to use the very unstable nature of the land as a stepping-off point for his design.

Killen's design placed an inverted gable roof on a series of canted walls and framed main living spaces on the ocean side with two-storey window walls. Since the house was built on a fairly steep slope, Killen designed a long, see-through glass bridge from the entry into the main living space, creating a Piranesian sense of drama. The main living spaces overlook an enormous lap pool, a preternaturally green lawn and the Pacific Ocean a few hundred metres away. The inverted gable roof stretches from 1 to as far as 2.5 metres (3 to 8 feet) beyond the wall line, creating a natural shade for the strong afternoon sun. It also became a rain catcher funnelling rainwater into an underground cistern to be used later for landscape irrigation. Significant rigid steel framing and poured-in-place concrete buttressing provided resistance to any potential seismic event.

The exterior stucco walls were painted in sand-coloured hues mimicking the beach just steps away. Sitting by the pool, one can enjoy the spectacular and uncompromising view of the ocean and remember that Malibu was a place long before it was the eponymous automobile.

Photography by Charles Chesnut and Aaron Killen

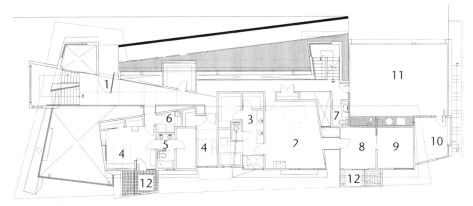

Second floor

First floor

1 Entry
2 Master bedroom
3 Master bathroom
4 Bedroom
5 Bathroom
6 Laundry
7 Powder room
8 Meditation room
9 Yoga room
10 Office
11 Garage
12 Deck
13 Great room
14 Kitchen
15 Dining
16 Theatre
17 Gym
18 Gallery

Designed to Last

Australia // Swaney Draper Architects

The sound of surf fills this house at Lorne, overlooking Victoria's Great Ocean Road. The crashing waves literally appear to be at the doorstep. The architects excavated 4 metres (13 feet) on the relatively steep site to nestle the house between neighbours. And to ensure privacy from the winding coastal road, a 3-metre (10-foot) cantilevered deck was added.

The brief was to create a large home that took advantage of the vista over Loutitt Bay. While the outlook from the lighthouse at Airey's Inlet to the pier at Lorne is impressive, so is the windchill, particularly during the winter months. The architects created a more temperate environment with a protected rear courtyard as well as front decks. They were also mindful of not sacrificing water views for comfort and as a result, there are unimpeded views from the rear terrace and lawn through glass doors on either side of the living areas.

The house, clad in black-stained timber, features a striking 8-metre-high (26-foot) sandstone spine wall. Slicing the house into two, this wall also delineates the bedrooms from the living areas. Containing two fireplaces and areas for wood storage, the sandstone wall and hearth extend from the front deck and lounge to the rear courtyard, blurring the indoor and outdoor spaces.

The kitchen is placed to one side of the living area. The central island bench, made of stone, includes two sinks and occupies a premier position. The dining area features a cantilevered built-in window box. Externally framed by an aluminium 'picture frame', the seat with its large picture window is one of the most favoured spots in the house. Louvred blinds, operated automatically, ensure the amount of sunlight is controlled.

Spaces are carefully arranged over six levels. The children's play area, leading from the kitchen, is oriented to the north and rear courtyard. Featuring bi-fold glass doors, this room opens to a small patch of lawn. In contrast, the main bedroom occupies the top level of the house. Designed like a retreat, it features a built-in study at one end and an open-plan bathroom at the other.

This beach house has a timeless quality. 'It's not just about natural ventilation and using recycled materials. It's as important to design a building that lasts,' says architect Simon Swaney.

Photography by Trevor Mein

Second floor

First floor

Ground floor

Dramatic Views

USA // Eggleston Farkas Architects

This 232-square-metre (2500-square-foot) waterfront residence is located on a long and narrow site with views across Puget Sound. The house is set back from the water and elevated to protect the structure from storm-surge flooding. The topography of the site includes a steep slope, which although providing a pleasant buffering backdrop, is also a source for potential landslides. The existing house was replaced by a new building that establishes a simple, comfortable presence within this beach context.

The new residence was conceived as a mediating portal between hillside and waterfront. A massive, 3-metre-high (10-foot) concrete catchment wall was introduced near the bottom of the problematic slope to protect against landslides. The top of this wall serves as a starting point for a new steel-and-wood access bridge at the second-storey main level. This elevated position serves to enhance views from the integrated entry, living, dining, kitchen and deck spaces. The living area is a two-storey volume with full-height window walls facing both the hill and water. Its transparency provides a dramatic view from the access road and allows views of both the hillside and the beach.

For privacy and optimal views, a master suite was placed on the top level, directly above the kitchen and dining areas. The beach-level plan comprises two rooms designed to be used as media, office, guest and entertainment spaces. Cedar siding with exposed fasteners is used on the exterior walls and will weather to a silvery patina.

Photography by Jim Van Gundy and Alex Hayden

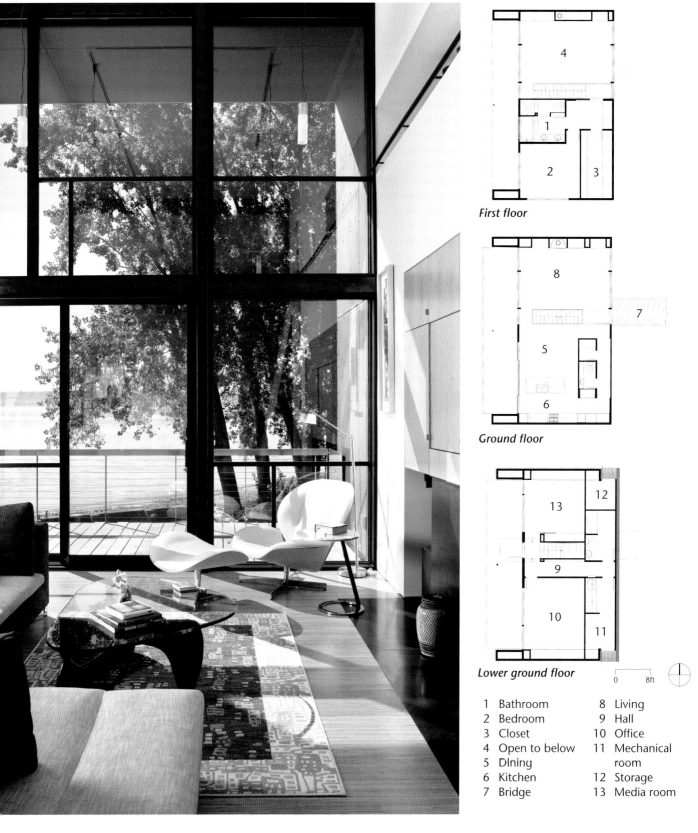

First floor

Ground floor

Lower ground floor

0   8ft

1 Bathroom
2 Bedroom
3 Closet
4 Open to below
5 Dining
6 Kitchen
7 Bridge
8 Living
9 Hall
10 Office
11 Mechanical
   room
12 Storage
13 Media room

151

Effortlessly Connected

Australia // Rolf Ockert Design

This house is located on a small but stunningly located site with panoramic views of the Pacific Ocean. To the east, the house opens up almost completely to large decks that overlook the water, with the sliding doors designed to allow many different configurations for the internal–external connection of spaces. A generous, open-plan living/dining/kitchen area at entry level is the central focus of the house, with the children's areas located below and the master bedroom above. A series of stairs, including the open, main stair running across the short length of the site, connects all levels effortlessly.

The centrepiece on the upper level is the freestanding bathtub in the middle of a room that offers uninterrupted views across the ocean. A large, curved sliding door closes off the otherwise open bedroom area for acoustic and visual privacy. The lower floor is the children's realm, comprising three large bedrooms and a play area with direct access to the lower garden and pool.

The main, middle level has a large kitchen, a dining area in its own protruding pocket, and the main seating area located under a curved void. Some design decisions, made on-site after experiencing the play of light through holes in the roof formwork as it was laid, resulted in design features that help define the house, such as the three skylights over the void and the hole-filled wall to the garage.

Photography by Sharrin Rees

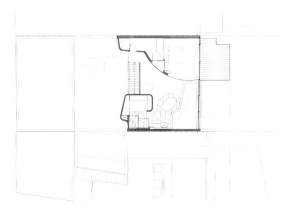

First floor

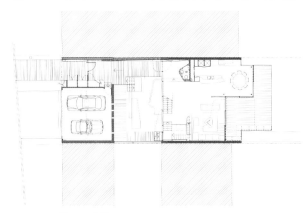

Ground floor

Lower ground floor

Extending the Natural Environment

Peru // Longhi Architects

This 511-square-metre (5500-square-foot) beach house, located 110 kilometres (70 miles) south of Lima, was conceived as a meeting point between the Peruvian desert and the Pacific Ocean. Sand garden roofs located on the eastern part of the house act as an extension of the desert, while lap and recreation pools on the western section provide a connection to the ocean. An in-situ concrete structure joins the architecture to the rocky cliff top as an extension of the natural environment.

The materiality of the house's components gives order to the design, transforming the natural to the artificial. For example, the natural rock at the lap pool area is sculpted to create a terrace bordered by natural rock, while the floor and steps are formed by crafted pieces of stone. A counterpoint to the connection between the natural rocks of the site and man-made architecture is found in the sophisticated use of a green stone sourced from the Peruvian Andes. The stone is used throughout the house and transitions from rough to fine when moving from exterior to interior.

Vertical circulation is provided by an open staircase, comprising stainless steel and timber steps, that cantilevers out from a wall finished with green stone. The house also includes a wine cellar and a living room located under the external swimming pool, where the exposed natural rock is accompanied by sophisticated architectural design. The glass box housing the living room, which offers a 180-degree view to the ocean and nearby cliffs, hangs from the structure to symbolise the relationship between sand and water.

Photography by CHOlon Photography

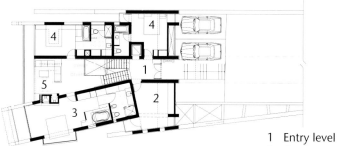

Entry level

1	Entry level
2	Study
3	Master bedroom
4	Bedroom
5	Family room

Main level

1	Living
2	Dining
3	Kitchen
4	Bedroom
5	Powder room
6	Patio
7	Wine cellar

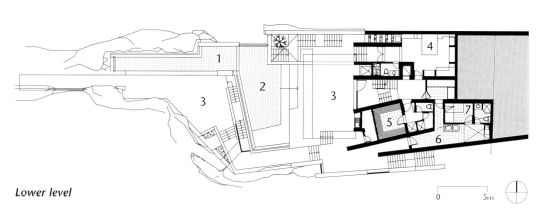

Lower level

1	Lap pool
2	Main pool
3	Terrace
4	Bedroom
5	Sauna
6	Service patio
7	Maid's room

0   5m

Highly-expressive Interiors

USA // Obie G Bowman

Located on a bluff-top lot with primary coastal views to the north and secondary coastal views to the south, this three-bedroom house includes an office, library, two-car garage, darkroom, and courtyard for a total of 232 square metres (2500 square feet) of heated space. The heavy timber-framed house bridges over the west side of a wind-protected courtyard to allow ocean views from the first-floor bedrooms and sitting room on the east side. A long corner solarium captures panoramic coastal views and sunlight while extending the living, dining and kitchen areas toward the ocean. Natural ventilation and cooling are provided via an array of automated air-intake vents and thermal exhaust chimneys.

The exterior walls comprise columns fixed to the foundation with horizontal girts bolted to them. Vertical decking spans between the girts with shear plywood, insulation, building paper, and redwood siding fastened to the exterior. The roof construction is similar   although thicker decking is used – and the end result is a wooden interior highly expressive of its structure and construction. All interior timber is Douglas fir, except for the floors, which are red ash. Floors on grade are exposed concrete or sun-dried Mexican pavers and the interior walls are painted gypsum wallboard.

Photography by Tom Rider

Inspired by Bali

USA // Olson Kundig Architects

Inspired by traditional Balinese palaces and temples, this contemporary residence is sited on a beautiful promontory of exposed lava. A river of hardened lava runs through the site, symbolically connecting the house to the great Hawaiian sources of energy – the mountains and the sea.

Though modern, the house uses tropical design concepts to fit naturally into its setting and to take advantage of time-honoured building practices. Broad overhangs protect the large expanses of sliding window walls from the sun, yet allow the house to be cooled by sea breezes. Windows are arranged to maximise cross ventilation, and a combination of shutters, screens and doors allow the owners to adjust the temperature inside.

A lava rock base anchors the house to the site, while the roof planes appear to float in the sky. The house is built with long-lasting materials – stone, teak, bronze, steel and copper – to stand up to the harsh coastal weather. The restrained elegance of the material palette serves as a quiet backdrop for the owners' collection of Asian art and artefacts as well as modern art.

Photography by Paul Warchol

Ground floor

1 Auto court
2 Courtyard
3 Entry
4 Gallery
5 Great room (living, dining, sitting)
6 Master bedroom
7 Den
8 Guest room
9 Kitchen
10 Terrace
11 Garage
12 Game room
13 Lanai
14 Pool

Inspired by Frangipani

Australia // Paul Uhlmann Architects

This beach house, designed by Paul Uhlmann Architects, occupies four regular-sized house blocks. 'My client started with two blocks of land. Two additional blocks became available. It was too tempting to resist,' says Uhlmann, who was able to provide a 200-square-metre (2150-square-foot) skate park on the extra land.

The owners, a couple with three children, wanted a house that made the most of the generous allotment. As a result, the house includes a kitchen, living and entertaining area at ground level, together with a media room, a playroom and a guest bedroom. On the first floor are five bedrooms and a library. And on the top floor is a gymnasium and an additional entertaining area, complete with its own wine cellar. 'I think it has just about everything you could possibly want,' says Uhlmann.

One of the main requisites in the design was to create a strong connection to the beach, which is directly in front of the house. The main living areas on the ground floor open up towards the ocean on the east, while the pool area is located in a protected northwest corner of the site. The bedrooms, suspended above, provide extra cover and protection for the pool deck. This ensures that the feeling of an outdoor living can still be enjoyed during strong south-easterly winds and rain. Once all the bi-folding doors are stacked open, the living areas become a covered deck space.

Unlike some beach houses that are constructed in lightweight materials such as timber, this home features concrete floors and block walls and a stone feature wall, the latter appearing both externally and internally. Aluminium slats also feature on the façade. 'We wanted to create a sense of arrival to the home. The slats also cover some of the equipment, such as an air conditioning unit,' says Uhlmann. One of the details in the home's interior can be traced to Fiji. 'The owners have strong ties to Fiji. We've used the frangipani motif extensively in the detailing.'

Photography by David Sandison

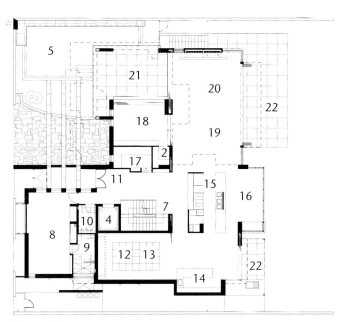

Ground floor

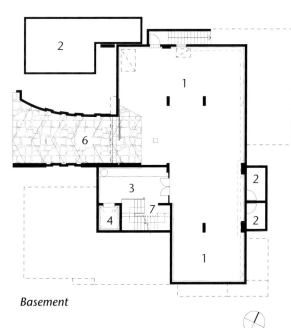

Basement

1 Garage
2 Store
3 Entry lobby
4 Lift
5 Pool
6 Driveway
7 Stair
8 Bedroom
9 Ensuite
10 Powder room
11 Entry
12 Media room
13 Dancing pole
14 Bar
15 Kitchen
16 Breakfast room
17 Study
18 Rumpus room
19 Dining
20 Living
21 Deck
22 Terrace

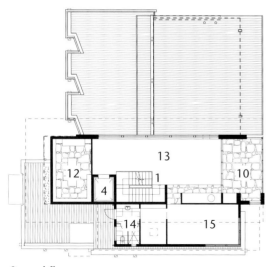

Second floor

First floor

1 Stair
2 Bedroom
3 Ensuite
4 Lift
5 Walk-in robe
6 Master bedroom
7 Library
8 Sitting
9 Laundry
10 Deck
11 Void
12 Cellar
13 Entertainment room
14 Bathroom
15 Gymnasium

Integrated with the Environment

Brazil // Gerson Castelo Branco

With wonderful views exploited by Gerson Castelo Branco, this house was designed for a business couple with three children as a weekend meeting place for family and friends. It is located where the ocean meets the dunes and the beautiful wide Uruaú Lagoon.

Taking advantage of the natural declivity of the land, Gerson's project places the viewer in a small private paradise without being monotonous – a fault of many of the old rural houses. The outlook from three levels captures the natural ocean breeze ventilation with no need for air conditioning.

Entry to the house is through the intermediate level, crossing a suspended ramp over a mirror of water. Openings ensure that the rooms below, including the kitchen, wine cellar, servants' rooms and bathroom, are all naturally ventilated. Also on this level are the swimming pool, sauna, the games room and a garage for cars and boats. The main entrance goes directly to the living room and the theatre room, which are enhanced by three belvederes that open to a beautiful exterior view.

The eucalyptus timber is one of the house's highlights, along with the roof's special timber: cavaco from Pará, a northern state of Brazil; and ipê, a Brazilian wood used for the doors and window frames.

The widespread use of glass allows a total integration with the rich local environment. At its highest point, the roof is like a delta wing or hang-glider shape, which is also one of the architect's registered landmarks and an important element of his architecture.

Photography by Tadeu Lubambo

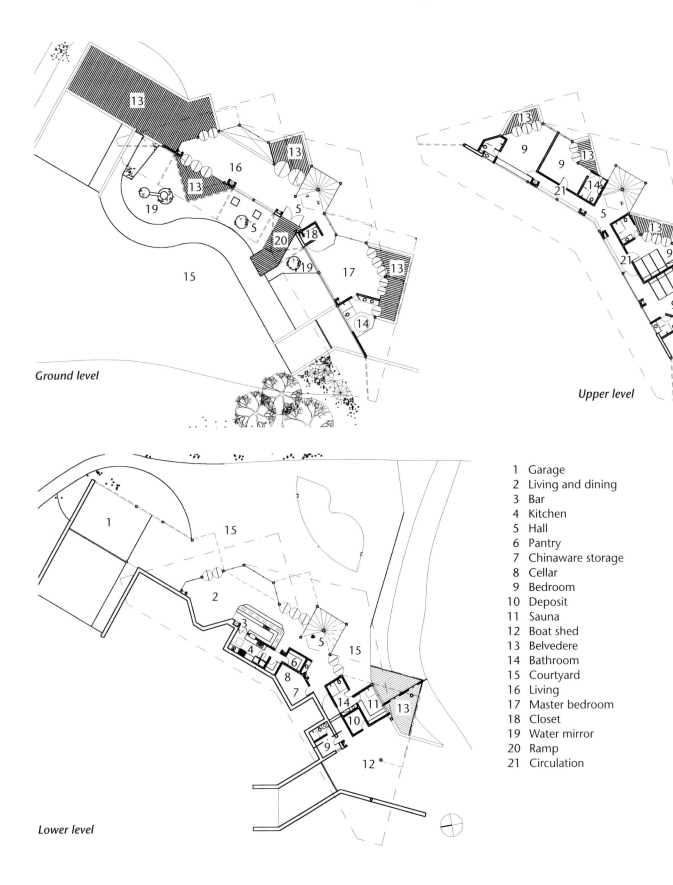

Ground level

Upper level

Lower level

1 Garage
2 Living and dining
3 Bar
4 Kitchen
5 Hall
6 Pantry
7 Chinaware storage
8 Cellar
9 Bedroom
10 Deposit
11 Sauna
12 Boat shed
13 Belvedere
14 Bathroom
15 Courtyard
16 Living
17 Master bedroom
18 Closet
19 Water mirror
20 Ramp
21 Circulation

Metamorphosis

Chile // Ulloa Davet + Ding

This striking, 175-square-metre (1900-square-foot) cliff-top house is the result of an extension and renovation of an existing structure. The existing roof has been transformed into a panoramic deck offering views along the coastline. This viewing deck is open to the public and is accessed via an independent stair.

The layout of the existing house was maintained and reinforced, and the south façade, located in the central area of the structure, was enlarged to provide a new living area with ocean views. A new bedroom is cantilevered over the entrance, with the absence of columns reinforcing the dynamics of the volume and protecting the space below from sun and rain. The addition is made from Oregon pine, while Radiata pine is used for the rest of the house.

The master bedroom, located in the lower east area of the house, was renovated to relocate a bathroom that obstructed the central circulation axis. To assist circulation, an additional entrance on the east façade allows a direct connection to the adjacent valley. The façade is designed as a ventilated skin that affords greater durability and thermal stability, protecting it from the harsh coastal conditions. The timber façade is constructed in a three-four rhythm, where every three planks change a module and every four modules change a set. This design generates a natural texture and is interrupted only by the square-shaped openings.

Photography by DD-JUD

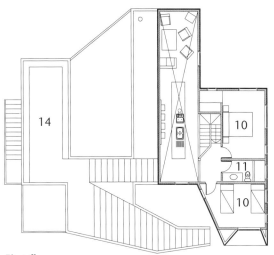

First floor

Ground floor

0   5m

1 Master bedroom	8 Kitchen
2 Ensuite	9 Living
3 East door	10 Bedroom
4 Breakfast terrace	11 Bathroom
5 Lounge	12 Main entrance
6 South sea-view terrace	13 Porch
7 Dining	14 Deck

Perched on a Slope

Greece // Alexandros N. Tombazis and Associates Architects

This 186-square-metre (2000-square-foot) house is built on a hillside overlooking the Gulf of Corinth. Due to the natural slope of the ground it was built over three levels – a basement with ancillary spaces, a ground floor comprising the main living spaces, and a mezzanine level above the kitchen – and resembles a cube perched on a sloping site.

The residence was developed according to bioclimatic design principles and has a solar chimney incorporated in its south façade. The main living areas create a unified open space and feature a two-sided, energy-efficient fireplace placed in the middle of the mezzanine railing, partly hanging over the living room. Special care was taken to ensure the gradual transition from interior to exterior areas. To achieve this, the architect oriented the verandahs toward both the sea and mountain views and positioned windows to allow natural lighting of all spaces throughout the day.

Fair-faced concrete was chosen for the exterior to better blend the building into the colours of the natural environment, and the roofs are planted. All interior walls are painted white and are complemented by various shades of grey throughout the house, punctuated by vividly coloured doors and furniture.

Photography by Alexandros N. Tombazis

Radically Remodelled

Australia // David Luck Architecture

This beach house, perched on a cliff, was originally built in the early 1980s. The brown brick, two-storey home, featured small windows that offered at best only glimpses of the water. 'We had to turn three bedrooms and two bathrooms into a five bedroom and four bathroom house,' says architect David Luck. 'It had to cater for a large family and all the relatives and friends staying over,' he adds.

Some of the extra bedrooms were accommodated by the removal of an indoor swimming pool. Several internal walls were also removed to make the spaces feel larger. One of the first walls to go was at ground level, removing a division between the front and rear doors. 'We wanted to create an unimpeded view to the backyard from the front entrance,' says Luck, who also increased the number of bedrooms on the ground level to three as well as providing two bathrooms, a family room and double garage.

The second level was also redesigned, particularly the original small apertures. Most of the brick walls were removed and substituted with floor-to-ceiling glass windows and large sliding doors. Luck also removed the 1980s timber balustrades that framed the house and substituted these with toughened framed glass. 'We wanted to ensure there was a view from wherever you stood in the house,' says Luck, who also included timber decks on all four sides of the upper level.

While the exterior was radically changed, including rendering the walls at ground level, rearrangement of the kitchen was minor. 'The kitchen has only been moved slightly. But the finishes have all been redone,' says Luck, pointing to the new timber and reconstituted stone central island bench.

The house now appears as a lightweight glass box floating on solid plinth. As Luck says, 'The idea was about inflating the spaces and the scale of the house. It now feels like a large viewing platform that draws your eye towards the horizon.'

Photography by Shania Shegedyn

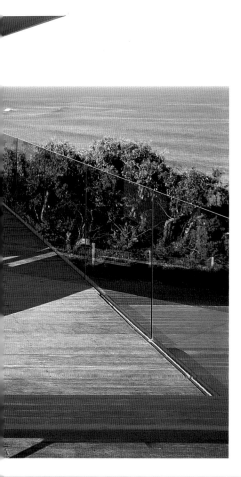

First floor

Ground floor

10

1 Deck	11 Entry
2 Living	12 Garage
3 Dining	13 Family room
4 Sitting	14 Studio
5 Kitchen	15 Bunkroom
6 Master bedroom	16 Gallery
7 Dressing room	17 Bedroom
8 Ensuite	18 Bathroom
9 Powder room	19 Laundry
10 Street	20 Store
	21 Back garden

Relaxed and Timeless

Australia // Max Pritchard Architect

Panoramic sea views and wind protection were strong design determinants of this spectacular holiday home. With an exposed site of sweeping views, the owners of this property required a relaxed holiday home that maximised views but still provided sheltered outdoor areas.

The house is elevated 1 metre (3 feet) above the ground to maximise the view and reinforce the dramatic form. The living area, with its dominant floating 'lid' roof, emphasises the drama of the exposed site. Two bedroom wings radiate from this core and enclose a rear, sheltered courtyard that features a wood-fired pizza oven. Indented timber decks placed either side of the living area provide further options for outside living and entertaining, with the choice dictated by wind direction.

Double-glazing and high-performance glass, cross ventilation and fans for cooling, and a highly efficient combustion heater have been used to minimise energy use, and hot water is obtained from an efficient electric heat pump. Corrugated colorbond, timber windows, flooring and decking reinforce the relaxed timeless holiday atmosphere, while the floating roof form adds drama to the exposed site.

Photography by Sam Noonan

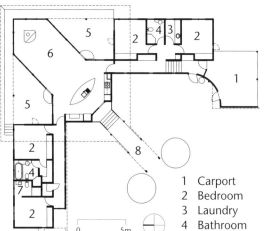

1 Carport
2 Bedroom
3 Laundry
4 Bathroom
5 Deck
6 Living, dining,
  kitchen
7 Ensuite
8 Rear courtyard

Retaining Charm

Uruguay // Diego Felix San Martín Lonne Arquitectos

'Stone House' is the result of the restoration and enlargement of a cement and stone house, which originally hosted a restaurant managed by the well-known Argentinean gourmand and designer, Mercedes Bosch. More recently, it has been converted into a family house. Its outstanding characteristic is the use of the original materials – stone and naked brick – that mark the house as an icon in the Punta Piedra region. The great challenge for the architects was to design a new project that met the client's need for a lighter and cosier visual appearance but didn't detract from the original character. They decided to replace the brick with the region's Lapacho wood, which develops a grey tone over time to match the yellowed ochre of the stone.

The original construction was located on a particular area of the Atlantic coast that exposed the local houses to the ocean at high tide. This meant the house was flooded two or three times a year, depending on storm activity. The best way to avoid floods was to elevate the ground floor and remove the existing reinforced concrete layer.

Prior to remodelling, the construction had the charm of an old ruin, and this was retained by the restoration, which joined the 'poetic' part of the ruin to the rest of the construction using natural Lapacho wood. There is an intrinsic dialogue between the external stones and the internal wood that was bought from an old warehouse in Montevideo port.

The triangular shape of the land has been followed in the restoration. The new area, which formerly housed the bedrooms, is connected to the main part of the house. The reception area and main entrance, the master bedroom and the music room, are linked through an internal corridor with open windows to the kitchen and the dining room.

The change in materials created a new modulation in the façades, which have turned their outlook to the engaging surroundings and ensure that many parts of the house have a view of Punta.

As well as meeting the client's requirements, the architects have captured the surrounding environment, invoking in both the interior and exterior the sensations evoked by wild natural surroundings.

Photography by Daniela MacAdden

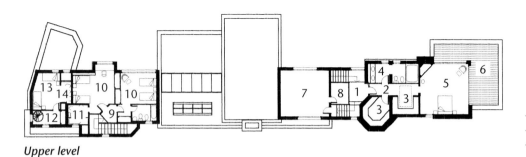

Upper level

1 Master bedroom hall
2 Master bedroom corridor
3 Closet
4 Bathroom
5 Master bedroom
6 Terrace deck
7 Music room
8 Storage
9 Corridor to bedrooms
10 Children's bedrooms
11 Children's bathroom
12 Service hall
13 Service bedroom
14 Service bathroom

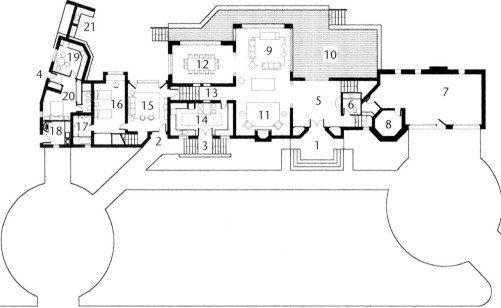
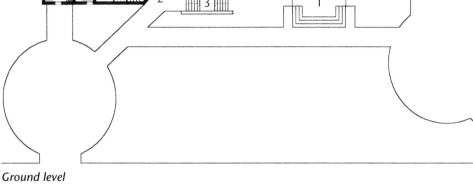

Ground level

1 Main access
2 Children's access
3 Service access
4 Tenant's access
5 Entrance hall
6 Toilet
7 Garage
8 Storage
9 Living
10 Terrace deck
11 Fireplace
12 Dining
13 Children's circulation
14 Kitchen
15 Children's living room
16 Children's bedroom
17 Children's bathroom
18 Bathroom
19 Tenant's living room/kitchen
20 Tenant's bedroom
21 Barbecue

T-shaped

New Zealand // Bossley Architects

Crashing surf makes its presence felt in this beach house and the noise of the surf competes with the strong winds. 'It's a fairly exposed site. There is not a great deal of vegetation for a windbreak,' says architect Pete Bossley, who designed this T-shaped house for a couple with four children.

While there are several beach houses along the shoreline, this house, perched high on the embankment, appears to be on its own. The T-shape was considered an appropriate response to the severity of the wind, allowing a more protected aspect behind the exposed living areas that embrace the site. The owners and guests arrive at a more sheltered part of the site and can park their cars undercover. A paved entrance leads past the children's bedroom wing and directly into the main pavilion that is divided between the kitchen, dining and living areas on one side and the main bedroom and guest bedroom and bathroom facilities on the other.

The living area leads to a large timber deck that features a 'catwalk' (a protruded walkway). 'We wanted to lead your eye out into the landscape. Even when the weather turns, it can be quite exhilarating to venture right out to the edge,' says Bossley, who says some of the most dramatic qualities of the home appear when a storm is about to break. 'We wanted to create the same excitement in the house,' says Bossley, who set up strong horizontal lines within the interior to create different perspectives of the hills and sea.

The beach house, which is made of steel and glass, features a lightweight skillion-shaped roof. And while the house appears relatively lightweight, especially in this environment, it is firmly anchored to the site by a rendered concrete plinth. As Bossley says, 'We saw the house as a viewing platform. It was designed to take a back seat to the landscape.'

Photography by Patrick Reynolds

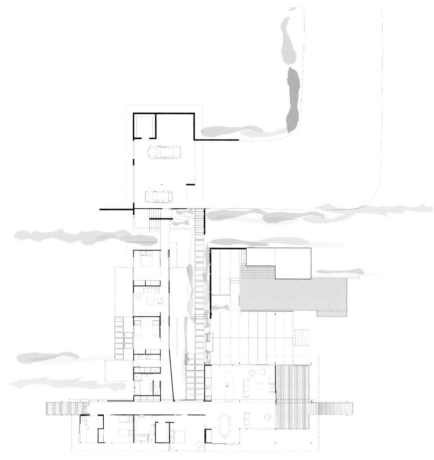

Floor plan

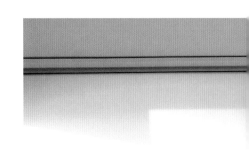

Unfolding Views

USA // Stelle Architects

This waterfront property unfolds in a sequence of views – both revealed and concealed – and was conceptualised as a kind of Kabuki shadow play that starts at the driveway and snakes down the entire length of the 2-hectare (5-acre) lot.

A narrow wooden boardwalk leads from the parking area up to and under the house, continues through a thicket of brambles, and ends at the beach.

All plant materials used in the project were native species and have been orchestrated for maximum effect, and sand has been sculpted into wind-blown mounds surrounding the house. The main level is a 27.5-metre (90-foot) slab of glass and steel raised to gain water views and summer breezes. Specially fabricated screens of horizontal teak lattice break up the expanse of glass and serve as **brise-soleils**, blocking the sun along the south side and providing privacy. A staircase is subtly concealed behind another wall of lattice and leads up to the main living area.

Inside, the house is furnished with Spartan restraint, ensuring that the views of water and wild sunsets are the real decoration. The central living area has been geared for entertaining with freestanding kitchen islands and a seating area clustered around a fireplace. A master bedroom suite lies to the east while guest rooms and a bathroom are located to the west. The central living area extends out towards a terrace with a swimming pool that spills over the edge of a retaining wall to form a gently splashing waterfall. In a protected corner beneath the house is a terrace with an open-air fireplace that provides shelter on rainy, blustery days.

Photography by Jeff Heatley

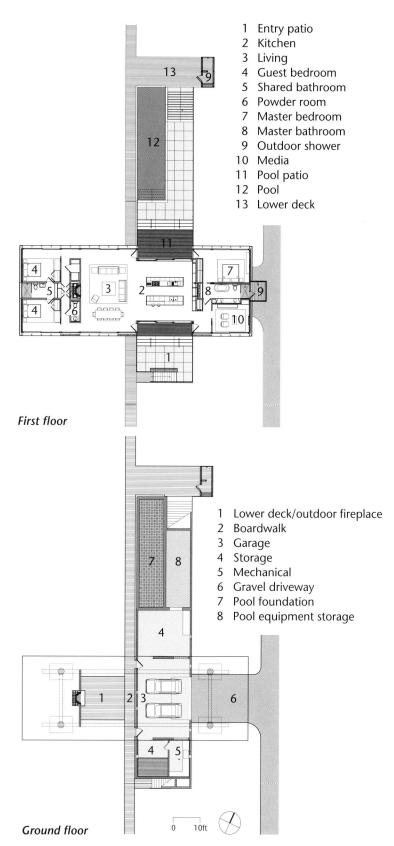

1 Entry patio
2 Kitchen
3 Living
4 Guest bedroom
5 Shared bathroom
6 Powder room
7 Master bedroom
8 Master bathroom
9 Outdoor shower
10 Media
11 Pool patio
12 Pool
13 Lower deck

First floor

1 Lower deck/outdoor fireplace
2 Boardwalk
3 Garage
4 Storage
5 Mechanical
6 Gravel driveway
7 Pool foundation
8 Pool equipment storage

Ground floor

0   10ft

Wide Bay Views

New Zealand // Godward Guthrie Architecture

The exposed location of this beachfront property required the architect to ensure privacy from the adjoining coastal public walkway and provide adequate shelter from the wind and sun. To achieve this, the main indoor and outdoor living spaces were conceived as a detached raised pavilion, placed high enough to achieve views to the bay but low enough to ensure an easy connection to the lawn and beach path beyond. The living area is almost entirely wrapped in sliding, full-height glazing panels that open onto a beach-facing terrace to the northeast and a sheltered courtyard behind. An exterior stair leads from the courtyard up to a large roof-deck living space, which offers wide views to the bay.

Sleeping areas are located in three separate zones – the children's rooms adjoining the lawn, the parents' area on the second level, and the guest rooms located above the garage. All rooms utilise a system of sliding glazed openings behind a layer of sliding, adjustable louvre screens. Cavity sliding doors are used throughout the interior of the house, some of which are automated, as is the pivoting front entry door that is fabricated from a huge single sheet of aluminium. In the living pavilion, the screens slide vertically up to the roof deck level, enabling the room to be opened entirely to the exterior, closed down fully to a shining metal case, or any variation between. Similarly, a pair of sliding, frameless glass panels allows the living area to be fully or partially connected to the rest of the house, or completely detached by the courtyard space.

This adjustability, along with flush floor tiling throughout, serves to minimise distinctions between internal and external space.

Photography by Patrick Reynolds

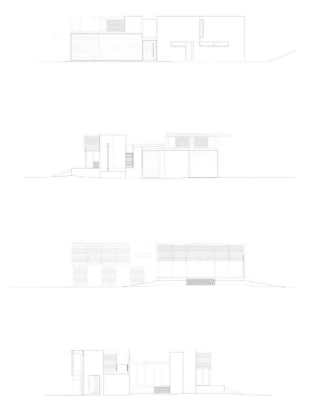

Elevations

Index of
Architects